Go to: https://www.elliejanderson.com for gardening tips, chicken coop plans by Erin Scott, short fiction, poetry, and excerpts from my novel.

ACKNOWLEDGEMENTS:

With thanks to Heather Kern, my first reader, editor, and formatting advisor.

With special thanks to Frances S. Dayee, my friend and editor.

And special thanks also to my husband, Shane Anderson, for technical support and photos.

Introduction

I grew up in the Rocky Mountains of southern Alberta. They call the province "sunny" but it is a brutal climate for gardening. Winter temperatures can reach 40 degrees below zero, and that doesn't account for wind chill. It often snows every month. It is a testament to the human spirit that anybody ever plants anything. Maybe that's why I remember so vividly the miracle of purple crocuses blooming through a lens of ice, the brilliant crimson of an Oriental poppy against the backdrop of a split-rail fence and snow-covered mountains. The whole family went out to look at them when they bloomed. It was such a miracle that they came back every year.

My grandparents owned a farm on the edge of Waterton , the Canadian side of Glacier National Park. My grandmother was an avid gardener and I followed her around. She wore a housedress, gumboots, and a white shawl with a silver thread woven through it. Sometimes, she draped the shawl over the fence, where the crows worried out the silver threads.

When I was seven, my grandmother gave me a bowlful of seeds to plant in the garden, a plot the size of a football field. I held the round, brown seeds and doubted they would ever turn into anything. But I admired my grandmother and trusted her. I still remember and relish my surprise when I grew a row of turnips. So white and purple, so absolutely beautiful. I didn't really like turnips, but I ate them anyway. I had grown them myself!!

When I was fifteen and had been told not to get in cars with boys, I went straight out and did just that. It was a silly thing to do when you live in a small town and come from a big family on both sides. My mother had nine siblings and my step-dad had eight, so I was related to almost everyone in town. The odds of someone seeing me were very high. But, at fifteen, I knew everything. I rode in that car for twenty minutes and by the time I got home, my mother knew all about it. I was grounded. For punishment, I was sent to the farm for the weekend to work. My grandmother took me to a hillside where she had a crop of potatoes. She dropped me off

had a crop of potatoes. She dropped me off
with a shovel, a pile of gunny sacks, a lunch,
a big bottle of water, my book, and the dog.

It was sunny and warm. The Quaking
Aspens glittered in the tiny, cooling breeze.
I carefully dug the potatoes and filled the
burlap sacks. Then I shared my lunch with
the dog and laid back in the grass to read.
Ultimately, the disciplinary measure of
forcing me to dig potatoes was not a
punishment. That day stands out in my
memory as one of the finest days of my life.

I'm a grown up, now, and have grown
children. I own the ratty white shawl with
the silver threads my grandmother wore. I
still dig in the dirt. My heart still lifts when
my irises bloom. I'm not the kind of
gardener who collects rare plants. I
celebrate the miracle of common
perennials.

As a home-owner with a full-time job and an active social life, I always wanted to be a better-organized gardener. I kept lists of tasks that needed to be done each month. I kept a journal and wrote things on a calendar. It felt scattered. So, I assembled this book from a box-full of chicken-scratched notes, newspaper clippings, and magazine articles I collected for more than thirty years.

This book contains a task list for each month, followed by blank pages for keeping notes. I hope you'll take this book into the garden. I hope it is blessed with fertilizer and dirt. Here, you can record the basics of your gardening life:

- Planting dates
- Germination dates
- Beginning and end of harvest
- Bloom periods
- Vegetable and flower varieties, including performance
- Dates of garden tasks like fertilizing, watering, spraying, and pruning
- Costs of plants and supplies
- Location of plants

Hellebore

January 2023

Sun	Mon	Tue	Wed	Thu	Fri	Sat
1	2	3	4	5	6	7
8	9	10	11	12	13	14
15	16	17	18	19	20	21
22	23	24	25	26	27	28
29	30	31				

Regular Garden Chores
- Weed
- Rake
- Control slugs

Plant
- Transplant trees and shrubs, vines, roses, perennials, ground covers, berries, artichokes, asparagus, horseradish, rhubarb
- Plant amaryllis bulbs indoors

Prune
- Prune trees and shrubs
- Cut back ornamental grasses
- Trim hedges
- Check stored bulbs

Fertilize
- At the end of the month, fertilize artichokes, asparagus, rhubarb, berries, grape vines
- Water winter-stored geraniums and fuchsias
- Fertilize emerging perennials and bulbs with bone meal or compost
- Fertilize newly transplanted trees and shrubs

Lawn
~Avoid walking on the lawn

Other
- Feed the birds
- Dormant spray fruit trees (second time)
- Mulch the roses

Journal

_____

_____

_____

_____

_____

_____

_____

_____

_____

_____

_____

_____

_____

_____

Winter Heather

February 2023

Sun	Mon	Tue	Wed	Thu	Fri	Sat
			1	2	3	4
5	6	7	8	9	10	11
12	13	14	15	16	17	18
19	20	21	22	23	24	25
26	27	28				

Regular Garden Chores
- Weed
- Control slugs
- Turn the compost

Plant
If soil is not too wet, plant:
- Sweet peas and edible peas
- Spring-blooming perennials and rockery plants
- Asparagus and rhubarb
- Bare-root trees, shrubs, vines, and cane berries
- Primroses, pansies, azaleas, bulbs, and camellias
- Pansies, China phlox, sweet William, sweet alyssum, snapdragons and calendula

Prune
- Cut roses back a third to half of the new growth
- Deadhead hydrangeas and fertilize
- Prune fruit trees and grape vines

Fertilize
- Fertilize deciduous trees and shrubs. Use one small handful of lawn fertilizer per foot of height.
- Add compost to the garden
- Repot, groom, and fertilize houseplants
- Feed lilacs

Lawn

- Dethatch and aerate the lawn
- Apply moss control to the lawn
- Apply lime to the lawn (must be done thirty days before fertilizing)

Other

- Dormant spray fruit trees (third time)
- Spray the roses regularly to control diseases.

Note: In the northwest, roses are particularly susceptible to blackspot and mildew. Also, they can become immune to the same spray, so remember to alternate sprays. There are several commercial products available. Some folks swear by bicarbonate of soda and water.

- Water all plants in dry areas such as under the eaves
- Begin spring clean up

Journal

_____

_____

_____

_____

_____

_____

_____

_____

_____

_____

_____

_____

_____

_____

Crocus

March 2023

Sun	Mon	Tue	Wed	Thu	Fri	Sat
			1	2	3	4
5	6	7	8	9	10	11
12	13	14	15	16	17	18
19	20	21	22	23	24	25
26	27	28	29	30	31	

Regular Garden Chores

- Weed
- Control slugs
- Turn the compost

Plant the following:

- Bulbs, corms, and tubers such as acidanthera, calla lily, crocosimia, gladiolus, ranunculus, and tigrida
- Peas and sweet peas, beets, cabbage, carrots, radishes, lettuce, potatoes, and chard
- Perennial vegetables like artichokes, asparagus, and rhubarb
- Seeds for calendula, clarkia, cosmos, godetia, larkspur, Shirley poppy, snapdragon, and sweet alyssum
- Direct sow seeds for perennial hardy Arabis, columbine, coral bells, delphinium, and veronica
- Sow tomato and squash seeds indoors
- Lilies
- Berries
- Groom and divide perennials; plant perennials
- Propagate chrysanthemums
- Last chance to transplant evergreens, shrubs, and vines

Prune

- Prune roses
- Trim and shape hedges
- Cut suckers
- Prune and feed summer-blooming clematis
- Cut back aging herbs like sage, rosemary, mint, thyme, and savory by one-half

Fertilize

~Fertilize evergreens, roses, and berries

Lawn

~Top-dress and over-seed established lawns

Other

- Spray the roses regularly to control diseases. Refer to the note on page 14.
- Water over-wintered plants and feed mid-month

Journal

_____

_____

_____

_____

_____

_____

_____

_____

_____

_____

_____

_____

_____

_____

Tulips

April 2023

Sun	Mon	Tue	Wed	Thu	Fri	Sat
						1
2	3	4	5	6	7	8
9	10	11	12	13	14	15
16	17	18	19	20	21	22
23/30	24	25	26	27	28	29

Regular Garden Chores

- Weed
- Control slugs
- Turn the compost
- Deadhead flowers

Plant the following:

- Beets, carrots, lettuce, endive, parsley, parsnips, peas, radishes, spinach, Swiss chard, turnips, and onions
- Seed potatoes
- Summer bulbs, corms, and tubers such as dahlias, gladiolus, acidanthera, callas, crocosima, ranunculus, and tigrida
- Herbs and berries
- Annual seeds of asters, cosmos, marigolds, zinnias
- Transplant summer annuals
- Indoors, start seeds of eggplants, peppers, tomatoes, and annual herbs such as basil
- Indoors, start seeds of cleome, linaria, lobelia, petunias, snapdragons, sweet alyssum, and verbena
- Divide and plant perennials – daylilies, hostas and phlox
- Set out transplants of broccoli, Brussels sprouts, cabbage, cauliflower and onions

Prune

~Prune candles of conifers if needed

Fertilize

- Fertilize asparagus and rhubarb
- Fertilize azaleas and rhododendrons after they bloom
- Fertilize spring blooming bulbs with a mixture of bone meal and compost as they finish flowering

Lawn

- Rake moss and thatch lawn
- Over-seed the lawn
- Fertilize the lawn around April 15th.
- For lawns, apply fertilizer 4 times a year: Easter, 4th of July, Labor Day, and Thanksgiving

Other

- Take winter-stored fuchsias and geraniums outdoors
- Spray the roses regularly to control   diseases. Refer to the note on page 14.

Journal

_____

_____

_____

_____

_____

_____

_____

_____

_____

_____

_____

_____

_____

_____

_____

_____

Just Joey Tea Rose

May 2023

Sun	Mon	Tue	Wed	Thu	Fri	Sat
	1	2	3	4	5	6
7	8	9	10	11	12	13
14	15	16	17	18	19	20
21	22	23	24	25	26	27
28	29	30	31			

Regular Garden Chores

- Weed
- Control slugs
- Turn the compost
- Deadhead

Plant the following:

- Summer bulbs
- Perennials: daylilies, hosta, penstemon, Siberian iris.
- Annuals and biennials such as African daisy, calendula, clarkia, cleome, cosmos, forget-me-not, godetia, linaria, lobelia, nasturtiums, pansies, portulaca, sunflower, snapdragons, sweet alyssum, sweet William, verbena, violas, and zinnia
- Tomatoes, peppers, basil, corn, squash, and beans late in the month
- Container-grown trees, and shrubs
- Vines: clematis, climbing hydrangea, wisteria
- Dahlias, gladiolus, calla lilies, chrysanthemums (plant gladiolus every two weeks)
- Divide summer-and-fall blooming perennials
- Fill containers with annuals and herbs
- Transplant annuals

Prune the following:

- Rhododendrons, azaleas, forsythia, clematis, and daphne
- Lilacs
- Wisteria as it finishes blooming
- Deadhead rhododendrons
- Pinch back perennials and annuals

Fertilize the following:

- Roses, evergreens, annuals, azaleas and rhododendrons
- Potted plants and vegetable garden every week

Other:

- Take cuttings from evergreens, shrubs, perennials, and houseplants
- Cut strawberry runners to keep the main plant producing strawberries. You can replant the runners if you want more plants.
- Spray the roses regularly to control diseases. Refer to the note on page 14.

Journal

_____

_____

_____

_____

_____

_____

_____

_____

_____

_____

_____

_____

_____

_____

_____

Siberian Iris

June 2023

Sun	Mon	Tue	Wed	Thu	Fri	Sat
				1	2	3
4	5	6	7	8	9	10
11	12	13	14	15	16	17
18	19	20	21	22	23	24
25	26	27	28	29	30	

Regular Garden Chores

- Weed
- Control slugs
- Turn the compost
- Deadhead

Plant the following:

- Beans, beets, corn, cucumbers, eggplant, melons, peppers, squash, tomatoes, and turnips
- Clematis and other vines
- Sunflowers
- Lettuce, spinach, and radishes every two weeks
- Perennials such as aster, artemisia, blanket flower, chrysanthemum, columbine, coreopsis, delphinium, erigeron, feverfew, foxglove, gilia, heuchera, hosta, Oriental poppy, penstemon, perennial sweet pea, potentilla, purple coneflower, salvia, and golden or purple sage
- Summer annuals: ageratum, celosia, cleome, cosmos, four-o'clocks, geraniums, marigold, nasturtiums, sunflower, sweet alyssum, portulaca, red salvia, and zinnias.
- In shade, plant begonias, coleus, forget-me-nots, and impatiens.
- Dahlias and gladiolus
- Dig and divide tulip bulbs
- Canna, montbretia, tigridia, and tuberous begonia
- Herbs
- Set out bedding plants

Prune
- Clip hedges
- Remove suckers

Fertilize
~Fertilize potted plants and vegetable garden weekly

Other
- Eliminate blackberries and horsetails
- Groom rhubarb
- Stake tall plants
- Thin fruits and vegetables
- Spray the roses regularly to control diseases. Refer to the note on page 14.

Journal

_____

_____

_____

_____

_____

_____

_____

_____

_____

_____

_____

_____

_____

_____

_____

Hydrangea

July 2023

Sun	Mon	Tue	Wed	Thu	Fri	Sat
						1
2	3	4	5	6	7	8
9	10	11	12	13	14	15
16	17	18	19	20	21	22
23	24	25	26	27	28	29
30	31					

Regular Garden Chores

- Weed
- Control slugs
- Turn the compost
- Deadhead

Plant the following:

- Fall crocus
- Divide bearded irises and poppies
- Lettuce, spinach, and radishes every two weeks
- Sow cosmos for September bloom
- You can still add annuals such as marigolds, salvias, and zinnias
- You can still direct-sow beets, broccoli, bush beans, carrots, chard, Chinese cabbage, kohlrabi, lettuce, scallions, peas, radishes, spinach, and turnips
- Replace faded annuals with celosia, marigolds, petunias, lantanas and verbenas
- Sow seeds of columbine, coreopsis, delphiniums, and rudbeckia

Prune

~Clean tattered foliage on perennials

Fertilize the following:

- Camellias.
- Potted plants and vegetable garden weekly.
- Roses
- Strawberries
- When ground covers finish blooming, clip them back, and fertilize

Other:

- Dig tulip, hyacinth, and narcissus bulbs
- Soak hanging baskets
- Spray the roses regularly to control diseases. Refer to the note on page 14.
- Take root cuttings of dianthus, marguerites, and Shasta daisies for planting in the fall
- For lawns, apply fertilizer 4 times a year: Easter, 4th of July, Labor Day, and Thanksgiving
- Take herb cuttings from new growth to transplant for use indoors during the winter

Journal

_____

_____

_____

_____

_____

_____

_____

_____

_____

_____

_____

_____

_____

_____

_____

_____

Rudbeckia

August 2023

Sun	Mon	Tue	Wed	Thu	Fri	Sat
		1	2	3	4	5
6	7	8	9	10	11	12
13	14	15	16	17	18	19
20	21	22	23	24	25	26
27	28	29	30	31		

Regular Garden Chores

- Weed
- Control slugs
- Turn the compost
- Deadhead

Plant

- Divide and plant early perennials such as bearded irises and Oriental poppy
- Plant fall vegetables like spinach, kale, chard, peas., radishes, and garlic
- For fall bloom, plant fall-flowering bulbs such as autumn crocus, lycoris, nerine, colchicum, and sternbergia

Fertilize

~Fertilize potted plants and vegetable garden every week

Lawn

~Control lawn weeds

Other

~Spray roses regularly to control diseases. Refer to the note on page 14.

Journal

_____

_____

_____

_____

_____

_____

_____

_____

_____

_____

_____

_____

_____

_____

_____

_____

_____

Orchid Dahlia

September 2023

Sun	Mon	Tue	Wed	Thu	Fri	Sat
					1	2
3	4	5	6	7	8	9
10	11	12	13	14	15	16
17	18	19	20	21	22	23
24	25	26	27	28	28	30

Regular Garden Chores

- Weed
- Control slugs
- Turn the compost
- Deadhead

Plant the following:

- Spring flowering bulbs – crocus, hyacinth, iris reticulata, daffodils, Siberian squill, and tulips
- Winter pansies, flowering kale, and cabbage
- Fall mums
- Perennials, trees, shrubs, and ground covers
- Arugula, beets, kale, kohlrabi, lettuce, peas, radishes, spinach, and mustard greens, for the last time this season
- Herbs like parsley, cilantro, chervil, chives, thyme, and sage for winter and spring harvests
- Asters, boltonia, snapdragons, pansies, and chrysanthemums
- Bare-root bearded irises and lilies
- Sow seeds for asters, bee balm, baby blue eyes, calendula, clarkia, candytuft, catmint, columbine, coreopsis, dianthus, holly hock, godetia, larkspur, pansy, phlox, poppy, rudbeckia, snapdragon, sweet alyssum, stock and violets
- Dig, divide, and replant irises and overcrowded clump-forming perennials
- Take perennial cuttings for propagation
- Force bulbs for Christmas gifts – amaryllis and narcissus
- Dig and divide daffodils

Prune

- Cut out raspberry canes that produced this year. Tie up the new canes and top them at five feet.
- Root-prune wisteria that has failed to bloom. Cut a complete circle 3' from the stem and fertilize with a high-phosphate fertilizer.

Fertilize

~Fertilize pots, annuals, and vegetable garden every two weeks

Lawn

- Over-seed the lawn before the equinox
- Spray the lawn for weeds
- For lawns, apply fertilizer 4 times a year: Easter, 4th of July, Labor Day, and Thanksgiving

Other

- Clean thoroughly around roses
- Rake leaves
- Cut everlasting flowers such as statice and globe amaranth and herbs for drying
- Start cleaning vegetable garden beds
- Take herb cuttings from new growth to transplant for use indoors during the winter
- Gather seeds of nasturtiums and marigolds
- On a warm day, spray the roses to control diseases. Refer to the note on page 14.

Journal

_____

_____

_____

_____

_____

_____

_____

_____

_____

_____

_____

_____

_____

_____

_____

_____

Succulent Groundcover

October 2023

Sun	Mon	Tue	Wed	Thu	Fri	Sat
1	2	3	4	5	6	7
8	9	10	11	12	13	14
15	16	17	18	19	20	21
22	23	24	25	26	27	28
29	30	31				

Regular Garden Chores:

- Weed
- Control slugs
- Rake
- Deadhead

Plant the following:

- Tulips and daffodils, alliums, scilla, anemones, crocuses, Dutch iris, freesias, galanthus, hyacinths, muscari, and ranunculus
- Evergreens, deciduous trees, shrubs, ground covers, and vines
- Berries, rhubarb and asparagus
- Sow seeds for asters, baby blue eyes, calendula, clarkia, candytuft, columbine, coreopsis, dianthus, holly hock, godetia, larkspur, pansy, poppy, rudbeckia, snapdragon, sweet alyssum, and stock
- Divide Siberian irises
- Sow wildflower seeds
- Divide and re-plant spring blooming perennials—any that are smaller or weaker than in years past, such as asters, callas, daisies, daylilies, hostas and Oriental poppies
- Plant pots for spring bloom
- Pot up herbs for indoor winter use

Prune

- Cut back old berry canes and trim new canes to six feet
- If there is a hard freeze, cut back perennials

Fertilize

~ Fertilize established bulb beds

Lawn

~Early in the month, over-seed the lawn

Other

- Harvest fruits and vegetables
- Mulch frost-tender bulbs, corms, and tubers
- Spray to control mildew and black spot on roses
- Clean thoroughly around roses
- Rake leaves
- Put the vegetable beds to bed for the winter
- Stop deadheading the roses to encourage dormancy
- Remove annuals
- Leave ornamental grasses and coneflowers for winter interest
- Feed the birds

Journal

_____

_____

_____

_____

_____

_____

_____

_____

_____

_____

_____

_____

_____

_____

_____

Purple Smoke Bush

November 2023

Sun	Mon	Tue	Wed	Thu	Fri	Sat
			1	2	3	4
5	6	7	8	9	10	11
12	13	14	15	16	17	18
19	20	21	22	23	24	25
26	27	28	29	30		

Regular Garden Chores

- Weed
- Rake
- Control slugs

Plant the following:

- Garlic
- Vines, trees, and shrubs
- Berries
- Camellias
- Peonies
- Paper White narcissus in pots every two weeks for continuous bloom
- Complete planting spring bulbs
- Finish planting wildflowers
- Divide lilies and replant
- Divide rhubarb. Leave at least one bud for each division. Replant 3 to 4' apart.

Prune

- Cut back chrysanthemums
- After the first frost, cut back perennials
- Prune trees and shrubs
- Cut back Butterfly Bush to 3'

Lawn

~Fertilize the lawn late in the month

Other

- Winterize tender plants
- Clean thoroughly around roses
- Rake leaves
- Remove all rose foliage
- Put away hoses and timers
- Feed the birds
- Take geranium cuttings
- Take geraniums and fuschias inside for the winter
- Move dormant amaryllis into light to begin a new growth cycle. Refresh soil. Start watering.
- For propagation, take hardwood cuttings of dormant plants such as forsythia, wisteria, willow, dogwood, potentilla, spirea, poplar, honeysuckle, and privet

Journal

_____

_____

_____

_____

_____

_____

_____

_____

_____

_____

_____

_____

_____

_____

_____

Humming Bird on Potato Vine

December 2023

Sun	Mon	Tue	Wed	Thu	Fri	Sat
					1	2
3	4	5	6	7	8	9
10	11	12	13	14	15	16
17	18	19	20	21	22	23
24/31	25	26	27	28	29	30

Regular Garden Chores

- Weed
- Control slugs
- Rake

Plant
~If the weather is mild, last chance to plant spring bulbs

Prune:
~Prune and shape trees

Fertilize
~Late winter --- top dress perennial beds with manure

Lawn
~Avoid walking on the lawn.

Other

- Mulch tender plants against the cold
- Strip the roses of leaves
- Rake leaves
- Clean, oil, and sharpen your garden tools.
- Add fireplace ashes to vegetable and perennial beds at the rate of a shovelful per square yard
- Propagate rhodendrons by ground-layering.
- Propagate from cuttings: aucuba, barberry, forsythia, holly, honeysuckle, hydrangea, rose, rose of Sharon, spiraea, and weigela.

Journal

_____

_____

_____

_____

_____

_____

_____

_____

_____

_____

_____

_____

_____

_____

_____

_____

Perennials for the Northwest – Full Sun

Ajuga reptans

Allium 3' - July bloomer

Alstroemeria

Alyssum – April blooming

Artemisia, silvery gray 2'-4'

Aster frikartii 'Monch' 3' lavender-blue flowers, sun -
    July bloomer

Aubretia – April blooming

Azaleas 'kurume' for red, 'exbury' for yellow,
    'robin hills' in two-toned pastels, April
    blooming and spreading 'satsukis' for late
    bloom.

Beebalm (Monarda) 3' to 4', with red, pink, violet, or
    white flowers in summer. Attractive to
    hummingbirds. Needs water.

Bergenia – April blooming

Blanket flower (Gaillardia x grandiflora 'Goblin')

Blue oat grass (Helictotrichon sempervirens)

Blue fescue

Callistephus chinensis 'Powder Puff'

Candytuft – May blooming

Cape fuschia (Phygelius) shrubby with pink, red, or
    pale yellow flowers, 4' Sun or light shade.

Catmint (Nepeta faassenii 'Walker's Low')

Lavender-blue flowers.

Centaurea cyanus

Chinese Witch Hazel

Chrysanthemum pacificum 18" Grown for it's silver
    lined foliage.

Clematis – May blooming

Columbine - – June blooming

Coral bell – May blooming

Coreopsis (Tickseed)– yellow, orange, maroon or red.

Corsican sandwort (Arenaria balearica)

Crimson flag (Schizostylis coccinea) 'Viscountess Byng'
– a rhizome, full sun.
Daisy – June blooming
Daphne Odoro -- Or easier to grow Daphne tangutica
and retusa.
Daylily – (Hemerocallis) June blooming
Delphinium (D. elatum) tall. June blooming
Dianthus or Pinks - May blooming
Diascia – low growing with coral, pink, or lavender
flowers. Full sun to part shade.
Epimedium – April blooming
False sunflower (Heliopsis helianthoides 'Prairie
Sunset') 6' by 3' summer to fall blooming
Festuca mairei
Fritillaria meleagris
Gaura lindheimeri – white or pink blossoms. Full sun.
Gentian – May blooming
Gerbera
Geum – May blooming
Globe thistle (Echinops ritro)– July blooming
Heuchera micrantha 'Palace Purple'
Hens-and-chicks (Sempervivum spp)
Helianthemum – May blooming
Hollyhock (Alcea rosea) 5'-9' pink to rosy red, white,
yellow, salmon, purple with amaranth or
mounding plants at the base
Hypericum
Joe Pye weed (Eupatorium purpurem) 8', attracts
butterflies
Iris – May blooming
Iris reticulate
Lavender – French lavender (Lavandula dentate) 2'-3';
Spanish lavender (L. stoechas) 1.5'-3' ; English
lavender (L. angustifolia) for fragrance, 4',
Lavandula angustifolia 'Munstead' . All need
loose, draining soil.

Leucanthemum x sukperbum 'Crazy Daisy'

Liatris scariosa 'White Spires' July blooming

Lithodora

Lobelia or Hybrid cardinal flower (Campanulaceae) 2' by 6", red, purple, or pink needs moisture

Lupine

Lychnis (L. chalcedonica) hairy leaves and tiny red or white flowers in midsummer – 3'

Lythrum – July blooming

Maltese cross (Lychnis coronaria) has magenta to crimson or white flowers.

Miscanthus sinensis 'Variegatus.'

Monarda didyma cv.

Nemesia fruticans – vanilla scented lavender with pink or white flowers. 1'

Northern sea oats

Ozark sundrops (Oenothera macrocarpa, formerly O. missouriensis or Missouri evening primrose) yellow ground cover

Pincushion flower (Scabiosa 'Butterfly Blue' and 'Pink Mist')

Penstemons

Pennisetum alopecuroides

Peony – May blooming

Phlox –3' to 5', red, pink, orange, purple, white and variegated. Fragrant. May blooming 'Nora Leigh'

Polyanthus – May blooming

Poppy – May blooming

Primula – April blooming

Purple Coneflower – July blooming

Rosa rugosa 'Polareis' 7', thrives in cool weather, 'Jen's Munk' 5' pink, hardly ever out of bloom, 'Rote's Meer', 3.5 'to 4' purply flowers good fall foliage, 'BellePoitevine' 5'-6',

'Charles Alanel' 1.5' carpet;
'Pierette', 'Fru Dagmar Hastrup' 4' best fall
colors of yellow, oranges, and scarlets; 'Dart's
Dash' for rose hips, 'Magnifica' 4' fragrant, '
Schnee Eule' white
Rudbeckia hirta or Black-eyed Susan
Russian sage (Perovskia atriplicifolia)
Salvia (S. greggii) 3' white and yellow to orange and
red. Or Mexican Bush Sage (S. leucantha) 4' tall
with velvety purple flower spikes.
Santolina – July blooming
Saxifrage – April blooming
Scaevola aemula – low growing with masses of
lavender-blue flowers.
Sedum
Stipa tennuisima.
Switchgrass (Panicum virgatum) –beautiful gold in
autumn
Viola – April blooming
Verbena (peruviana) – ground cover. Pink, purple, red,
and white. Verbena 'Homestead Purple' 18"
Veronica – 1' to 3' tall, red, blue, pink, and white. - July
bloomer (Veronica spicata)
Wisteria – May blooming
Yarrow (A. filipendulina) 4'-5' tall yellow. White-
flowered yarrow is invasive.

Perennials for the Northwest – Full Sun to Partial or Light Shade

Alchemilla Mollis 'Lady's Mantle' 12"-18" Beautiful way
        of holding drops of water, but re-seeds
        invasively.
Anemone Japonica
Aquilegia (columbine) 1'-3' Early summer.
        Needs water to keep foliage through summer.
Astilbe – July blooming
Azalea
Bee balm (Monarda didyma) - hummingbirds
Beard-tongue (Penstemon) tall - hummingbirds
Bergenia, evergreen B. crassifolia blooms January
        through February. Magenta, pink, white.
Bleeding heart (Dicentra)
Butterfly bush (Buddleia davidii) 15' blue, purple,
        white, or lavender flowers. Hummingbirds and
        butterflies love it. Considered a noxious weed
        in Western Washington because it reseeds.
Centranthus – 3' Blooms in summer. Considered
        invasive but great in pots. Red, pink, or white.
Cinnamon fern (Osmunda cinnamomea)
Coral Bells (Heuchera) low – attract hummingbirds
Delphinium grandiflorum 'Blue Butterfly'
Foam flower (Tiarella)
Geum – 6"-12" mounds. Yellow, orange, and red. May
        through late summer.
Goatsbeard (Aruncus)
Hemerocallis (daylily) 2' to 4'
Heuchera 'Plum Pudding' thrives in both sun and part
        shade.
Honeysuckle (lonicera) Vine - hummingbirds
Iris sibirica – Blue, purple, white.

Japanese forestgrass (Hakonechloa macra 'Aureola')
Ligularia (L. dentate and L. stenocephala. Both do well
in pots. 'Desdemona' has large, round purplish
leaves and daisy-like yellow blooms. 'The
Rocket' has missile-shaped yellow flower
clusters.
Lilies (Lilium) tall - - hummingbirds
Lungwort (Pulmonaria)
Lupine
Phlox - hummingbirds
Platycodon grandifloras 2.5' has blue, violet, soft pink,
or white star-shaped flowers
Potentilla nepalensis – 12" salmon-colored flowers
Purple coneflower (Echinicea purpurea)
– hummingbirds – June blooming
Rosemary (Rosmarinus officinalis) - hummingbirds
Rudbeckia (Black-eyed Susans) 'Goldstrum' 2-3'
Sage (Salvia) low - hummingbirds
Thalictrum (T. dipterocarpum) lacy leaves and violet
flowers with yellow stamens
Toad lily (Tricyrtis)
Valerian (Centranthus ruber) 'Pretty Betsy' –
hummingbirds
Weigela spring flowers – hummingbirds

Combinations:

Heuchera 'Plum Pudding' thrives in both sun and part
shade. In sun, plant it with Artemisia 'Powis
Castle' or Stoke's aster (Stokesia laevis) 'Klaus
Jelitto' has lavender blue flowers. 'Silver Moon'
is creamy white.
Lime green Choisya ternate 'Sundance', white
coneflowers, giant alliums, rose asters, and
variegated Pulmonaria 'David Ward.'

Perennials for the Northwest – Moist Shade

Ajuga
Angelica (Angelica archangelica) 4'-7' tall and 3' wide
Begonia
Bleeding Heart (Dicentra)
False Solomon's seal (Smilacina)
Hosta sieboldiana – blue-green leaves; H.
      lancifolia – dark green leaves.
Iris – Japanese or Siberian
Ligularia Purplish stems and foliage with golden
      yellow flowers 4' by 3'
Rodgersia 4' by 3'
Lobelia (Cardinal Flower) 'Queen Victoria' or 'Sparkle
      Devine" 2' to 4' H and 1' W
Monarda (Bee Balm) Red or pink 24" x 18"
Persicaria (Fleece Flower) 'Red Dragon' has burgundy
      leaves with small white flowers 'Fire Tail' has
      bright red flowers. "Painter's Pallete' is cream
      and red. 3' by 3'
Scrophularia auriculata 'Variegata' (Variegated Water
      Figwort) tiny wine-red flowers. 2' by 2'.
Solomon's seal (Polygonatum commutatum) 3' to 6'
Trollius (Globeflower) orange to yellow 2'-3' high and
      wide
Viola Labradoric (Labrador Violet) Purple leaves.
      36"X24" midsummer

Combinations:

Heuchera 'Plum Pudding' pairs well with Hakone grass
      (Hakonechloa macra 'Aureola'), hostas '
      Piedmont Gold' and 'Patriot.'
Scotch moss

Perennials for the Northwest - Dry Areas

Aaura lindheimeri – 4', 'Whirling Butterflies' – White
Agastaches
Apple blossom grass (Gaura lindheimeri)
Blue Mist (Caryopteris clandonensis) blue flowers
Catmint (Nepeta fassenii 'Six Hills Giant') blue flowers
Creeping baby's breath (Gysophila repens 'Rosea')
       groundcover with pink blooms
Cyclamen coum—white, or magenta. Likes dry shade.
Deschampsia caespitosa 2' evergreen arching grass
Desert four o'clock (Mirabilis multiflora)
Diascia 'Little Charmer'
Eragrostis curvula – grass
Erysimum 'Bowles Mauve' --- gets huge, then dies
Esyrinchium striatum 1' irislike perennial with blue
       blades and yellow flowers.
Euphorbias : Euphorbia myrsinites will trail down the
       bank. Euphorbia x martini grows 2'- 3' with
       brown centered chartreuse flowers in late
       winter.
Best Euphorbia – Euphorbia characias subsp wulfenii.
       5' to 6' tall. Chartreuse.
Gaura lindheimeri – white blooms
Hummingbird trumpet (Zauschneria californica aka
       Epilobium canum)
Ice plant
Indian Blanket (Gaillardia aristata)
Lavender (Lavendula spp.)
Lavender cotton (Santolina chamaecyparissus)
Mexican hat (Ratibida columnifera)
Mexican Daisy, Erigeron karvinskianus.
Osteospermum 'Cream Symphony'
Pencil plant, verbena bonariensis -purple haze. 4' to 6'

Purple smoke tree (Cotinus coggygria 'Purpureus'or
      (Cotinus coggygria 'Royal Purple')
Russian sage (Perovskia atriplicifolia) 3' blue flowers
Silver mullein (Verbascum bombyciferum)
Sulphur flower (Erigonum umbellatum)
Soapweed (Yucca spp.)
Texas sage (Salvia greggi)
Wild hyssop (Agastache cana. A. barberi)
Wormwood (Artemisia absinthium 'Lambrook Silver')
Evergreen herb, silver leaves 3'
Yarrow (Achillea 'Hoffnung' yellow ferny
Zauschneria

Combinations:

Hypericum with Asclepias tuberose, orange and yellow
daylilies, ornamental grasses, purple ruellias and
verbenas.
Large shrubby hypericums with 'Annabelle' hydrangea,
oakleaf hydrangea, Cimicifuga spp. , dark green dwarf
conifers, monkshood (Aconitum spp.)

Rock rose Cistus 'Sunset'-2", hot magenta pink flowers,
likes dry.
Looks nice with blue oat grass, Helictotrichon
empervirens and Artemisia 'Powis Castle' and Senecio
greyi (also called Brachyglottis 'Sunshine.'). This plant
can get large.

Rock garden plants

Alyssum spp.
Bellflower (Campanula spp.) variety of heights and
      colors
Blanket flower (Gaillardia x grandiflora) 'Goblin'
Candytuft (Iberis spp.) Evergreen
Catmint (Nepeta x faassenii) 'Walker's Low'
Cinquefoil (Potentilla neumanniana)
Crocus spp. Early spring flowers in many colors
Daylilies 'Stella d'Oro'
Groundcovers
Larkspur (Consolida ambigua) violet blooms in early
      summer
Lilies (Lilium spp.)
Love-in-a-mist (Nigella) 2'
Ozark sundrops (Oenothera macrocarpa, formerly O.
      missouriensis or Missouri evening primrose)
      yellow ground cover
Pinks (Dianthus spp.)
Poppies (Papaver spp.)
Salvia greggii 4' evergreen pink blooms in spring

Spring Interest Combinations

Pansies with grape hyacinths (Muscari)

Lady's mantle, with purple star of Persia (Allium christophii)

Red tulips (Tullipa fosteriana 'Robert Schuller') with Anemone blanda 'White Splendour'

Siberian bugloss (Brunnera macrophylla) and 'White Triumphator' lily-flowering tulips

Hardy cyclamen (Cyclamen coum) and 'Gemini' pansies (Viola x wittrockiana)

Primrose (Primula vulgaris) and Lent lily (Narcissus pseudonarcissus)

Trout lily (Erythronium revolutum) and lungwort (Pulmonaria angustifolia)

Tulips with Viburnum davidii and lime green Corsican hellebore (Helleborus argutifolius).

Golden arborvitae with bronze-foliaged Japanese barberry, feather reed grass and 'Frosty Morn' variegated sedum.

Pieris Japonica 'Mt. Fuji' Magnolia stellata, and yellow forsythia

'White Nancy' lamium with white feverfew, variegated scrophularia, and blue hydrangeas.

Marsh marigold (Caltha palustris) and forget-me-nots (Myosotis scorpioides)

Cushion spurge (Euphorbia polychrome) and yellow tulips

Honeywort (Cerinthe major) and star of Persia (Allium christophii)

Canna 'Tropicana' and Cosmos 'Diablo'

Crocosimia 'Lucifer' and daylily (Hemerocallis) 'American Revolution'

Bulb Combinations

What a thrill it is to see the first flowers of spring. When I was a kid in a coal-mining town, we had a neighbor who "planted" plastic tulips in her flower beds one spring. She couldn't have them any other way because of the ground freeze levels. In the Pacific Northwest, tulips flourish. I have some planted in a spot near the garage door that have bloomed profusely every year for ten years with no attention. The blooms were sparse this spring, so I will dig them up and re-plant them in the fall.

We do have rodents who like to transplant bulbs. One year I planted a hundred red tulips in one of my beds and then waited anxiously for them to flower. When the patch finally bloomed, I was surprised to see mysterious holes in the planting pattern. Then, I had an early Alzheimer's moment, when I found a patch of red tulips by the fence. I certainly didn't remember planting them there. Sure enough, when I dug them up, they had been piled in there. Probably a squirrel's stash.

The following list outlines various bulb combinations that are particularly striking.

February-March

Tulips Golden harvest' (yellow) or 'Pink Charm' (pink) with white wall rockcress (Arabis caucasica)

Tulips 'Golden Harvest' or 'Mount Hood' (white) with English primrose (Primula polyantha)

Tulips 'Romaine' (creamy white) or 'Mount Hood' underplanted with blue grape hyacinth (Muscari)

Dutch hyacinths 'Bismarck (white or blue) with white wall rock cress.

Tulips 'Mrs. John T. Scheepers' (yellow) with poppy-flowered 'Blue Poppy' anemone (A. coronaria) Narcissus, miniatures: 'Baby Moon', 'Tete a Tete' and 'February Gold'

Galanthus ikariae or G. elwesii 9"

Cyclamen coum – white, pink, or magenta. Likes dry shade.

Crosus tommasinianus 'Whitwell Purple' and 'Barr's Purple'

March-April

Ranunculus 'Apricot Shades' with blue Chinese forget-me-not (Cynoglossum amabile)

Tulips – 'Maureen' (white) with 'Blue Bunting' columbine (Aquilegia)

Mrs. John T. Scheepers with 'Blue Bunting' columbine (Aquilegia) or Siberian wallflower (Erysimum hieraciifolium)

'Pink Diamond' with 'Carmine King (pink) forget-me-not (Myosotis) or 'White Perfection' viola

'Sweet Harmony' (bright yellow) with 'Blue Bunting' columbine

'White Triumphator' with 'Blue Perfection' viola

Narcissus miniature, 'Minnow', 'Pencrebar'
Dog-tooth violets or trout lilies Erythronium 'Pagoda'
        has yellow flowers; E. revolutum has hot-pink
        flowers with yellow anthers.
Fritillaria meleagris, 1' prefers some shade white
        through purple-brown.
Angelica (Angelica archangelica) with spiderwort,
Penstemon, and tiger lily.

Alliums

Large: Allium 'Globemaster' 4' with 10" purple heads
Giant allium (a. giganteum) 5' with 5" purple heads
Medium sized: (A. aflatunense) 'Purple Sensation' 3'
        with 4" purple heads
Blue allium (A. caeruleum) 2' with 2" blue flowers in
        dense clusters
Drumsticks (A. sphaerocephalum) 2' with 2" reddish
        purple heads.
Star of Persia (A. christohii) 2.5'with 6" to 12" lavender
        heads
Short: A. neapolitanum – 1' with 3" flowers
Golden garlic (A. moly) 1' with 3" bright yellow flowers
Turkestan allium (A. karataviense) 8" stalks with
        flowers 4"

Summer Show

Artemisia lactiflora 'Guizhou' (white mugwort)
Astrantia major 'Sunningdale Variegated'
False sunflower (Heliopsis helianthoides) 'Prairie
     Sunset' 6' by 3'
Hypericum androsaemum 'Albury Purple'
Japanese anemone 'Honorine Jobert'
Lonicera periclymenum 'Belgica' (early Dutch
     honeysuckle) - vine
Lungwort (Pulmonaria)
Purple Coneflower
Masterwort
Salvia muelleri – royal purple
Siberian iris (Iris sibirica)
Trees: Stewartia pseudocamellia,
     Styrax obassia (fragrant snowbell)
Shrubs: Hydrangea paniculata 'Kyushu'
     rosa rubifolia (formerly Rosa glauca).
     Rosa rugosa 'Polareis' 7', thrives in cool
        weather
     'Jen's Munk' 5' pink, hardly ever out of bloom
     'Belle' Poitevine' 5-6'
     'Charles Alanel' 1.5' carpet
     'Pierette'
     'Dart's Dash' for rose hips
     'Magnifica' 4' fragrant
     'Schnee Eule' white

Summer Blooming Bulbs

Acidanthera (Gladiolus callianthus)
Baboon flower (Babiana stricta)
Blackberry lily (Belamcanda chinesis)
Blazing star (Liatris spp)
Caladium (Caladium bicolor)
Crinum (Crinum spp)

Calla lily (Zantedeschia spp.)
Canna (Canna x generalis)
Corn lily (Ixdia viridiflora)
Dahlia
Elephant ears (Colocasia esculenta)
Jacobean lily (Sprekelia formosissima)
Lily (Lilium spp. 'Miss Gaiety' orange, 'Cote d'Azur'
pink, 'Connecticut King' 3' yellow, 'Admiration'
white, 'Stargazer' crimson and white, "Black
Beauty' most disease-resistant, also blooms
from mid-summer into autumn; 'Chianti' red. '
'Casa Blanca', 'Mona Lisa' fragrant,
'Mediterranee' red, 'Le Reve' hot pink.'
Lily-of-the-Nile (agapanthus africanus)
Natal lily (Clivia spp.)
Nodding star-of-Bethlehem (Ornithogalum nutans)
Mexican shell flower (Tigridia pavonia)
Rain lily (Zephyranthes spp.)
Spider lily (Hymenocallis spp.)
Tuberous begonia (Begonia z tuberhybrida)
Wood sorrel (Oxalis)

Summer Interest Combinations
False sunflower (Heliopsis helianthoides 'Prairie
Sunset') 6'by 3' with Aster laevis 'Bluebird' 4'
and switch grass (Panicum virgatum 'Heavy
Metal') or dwarf fountain grass (Pennisetum
alopecuroides 'Hamelyn')
Phlox paniculata 'Becky Towe' with Rosa Mutabalis
and Melianthus major
Carex 'Frosted Curls' with annual hot pink candytuft
(Iberis umbellate)
Rudbeckia fulgida 'Goldsturm' and giant hyssop
Agastache 'Blue Fortune' – carefree
Colocasia 'Black Magic' with annual 'Purple Wave'
petunias and Plectranthus argentatus

Suggested Perennial Border

The number in brackets after the plant name is the suggested number of plants needed for the most impact.

Anemone Japonica (3) 'September Charm'
Centaurea Montana (2) 'Mountain Bluet' deep blue
      flowers
Centranthus Rubra (4) 2'-3'
Delphinium (3) choose 2 dark blues and a white.
Erigeron (3) Choose a pink one. 12"-18"
Hemerocallis (Daylily) (3) 'Stella de Oro' yellow.
Lavatera (1) 'Beardsly pink with a dark pink center 4'
Garden Phlox (1) 'Miss Lingard' white 3'
Rudbeckia (Black-eyed Susans) 'Goldstrum' 2'-3'
Salvia Superba (6) 'May Night' dark purple flowers.
      18"-20"

Suggested Perennial Garden

Coreopsis 'Limerock Ruby' (3)18" tall and wide
Yarrow (Achillea 'Paprika') (3) 2' tall and 18 " wide
Lambs' ears (Stachys byzantina) (6) 18" tall & 2' wide
Blue fescue (Festuca glauca)(5) 1' tall and 2' wide
Aster 'Purple Dome' (5)18" tall and 30" wide
Coreopsis 'Moonbeam' (3) 18" tall and wide
Bellflower (Campanula 'Blue Clips' (3) 8" tall, 12" wide,
Siberian iris ((Iris sibirica)(3) 4' tall and wide
Liatris 'Kobold' (3) 2' tall and wide
False indigo (Baptisia 'Prairie Smoke') (1) 4' tall
Purple coneflower (Echinacea purpurea) (3) 3'-5' tall,
      2' wide
Spiderwort (Tradescantia 'Osprey') (3) 2' tall, 15" wide
Feather reedgrass (Colomagrostis 'Karl Foerster') (3) 6'
      tall and 2' wide

South-Facing Hillside Garden

Trees, Shrubs and Perennials

Abelia grandiflora 'Edward Goucher'
Artemisia ludoviciana
Berberis thunbergii 'Rose Glow'
Caryopteris incana 'Bluebeard'
Cistus skanbergii
Cotinus coggygria 'Royal Purple'
Helichrysum angustifolium
Helleborus niger
Knautia Macedonia
Lavandula angustifolia
Rosa glauca
Senecio greyii

Underplantings

Ajuga 'Burgundy lace'
Fragaria chiloensis
Iberis
Origanum spp.
Salvia officianalis 'Tricolor'
Scilla
Silene schafta
Thymus spp.

Meadow Garden

Joe-Pye weed (Eupatorium maculatum) 'Gateway' (4),
    4' to 6' tall and 3' wide.
Purple coneflower (Echinacea purpurea) 'Bright
    Star' (8), 3' by 2'
Butterfly weed (Asclepias tuberose) (3) , 3' by 18"
Little bluestem grass (Schizachyrium scoparium) (12)
    3' clumping.
Spike gayfeather (Liatris spicata) (4), 3' by 18"
Plains coreopsis (Coreopsis tinctoria) (20),
    3' by 2' annual.

Mediterranean-Style Garden

Allium sp. 9" to 3' lilac, blue, rose or white. Poor soil,
    little water.
Artemisia spp. 2'- 4' Silver foliage
Ballota pseudodictamnus 2' mounder with silver-green
    leaves
Euphorbia myrsinites 1' groundcover with chartreuse
    spring blooms
Hebe cupressoides evergreen shrub 3'
Melianthus major 5' shrub
Santolina chamaecyparissus 2' mounder
Sedums spp
Wooly Thyme (Thymus pseudolanuginosus) 3"
Windmill palm (Trachycarpus fortunei)
Yucca spp 3' to 10' tall

Sunny, Damp Combinations

Lobelia or Hybrid cardinal flower (Campanulaceae)
    2" by 6", red, purple, or pink
Hardy hibiscus (H. moscheutos, Ho. Coccineous)
Turtleheads (Chelone spp.)
Ligularia dentate
Maiden grass (Miscanthus sinensis)

Cottage Garden Plants

Tall plants

Big bluestem (andropogon gerardii) 8' pale yellow
        blooms July to September
Bowman's root (Veronicastrum virginicum),
Boltonia (Boltonia asteroids) 5', white, pink, blue
        blooms July to October
Blue giant hyssop (agastache foeniculum) 4' blue
        blooms July to September
Canna (Canna spp.) 8' yellow, red, orange blooms July
        to October
Cardinal flower (Lobelia cardinalis) 5' red blooms July
        to September
Castor bean (Ricinus communis) 12', annual. Greenish
        blooms, June to October
Compass plant (Silphium laciniatum) 10' yellow
        blooms, July to September
Coneflower (Rudbeckia nitida 'Goldquelle' or Echinacea
        purpurea), 4' reddish purple blooms June to
        October
Cup plant (Silphium perfoliatum) 8' yellow blooms, July
        to September
Delphinium (elatum) 6' to 8' white, pink, lavender,
        purple, and blue blooms in early summer
Elephant's-ear (colocasia spp.) 5' green foliage July to
        September
Eulalia grass (Miscanthus sinensis) 8', white blooms
        August to September
False sunflower (Heliopsis helianthoides)
        'Prairie Sunset') 6' by 3' July to October

Fireweed (Epilobium angustifolium, 7' pink,
        purple, white blooms July to September
Foxgloves, Foxy strain (Nicotiana alata or Digitalis
        purpurea), 5' white or purple blooms July to
        September
Globe thistle (Echinops exaltatus)
Hollyhock (Alcea rosea) 5'-9', pink to rosy red blooms
Indian grass (Sorghastrum nutans) 6' green or yellow
        blooms July to September
Japanese burnet (Sanguisorbia obtusa),
Joe-pye weed (Eupatorium fistulosum)'Gateway'or
        (Eupatorium maculatum) 7' by 3'
Lupine Russell Hybrids (Lupinus spp.) 5' blue, pink, or
        white blooms May to June
Maiden grass (Miscanthus sinensis 'Gracillimus')
Meadow rue (Thalictrum rochebrunianum)
Pampas grass (Cortaderia selloana) 8' by 3'
Patrinia (Patrinia scabiosaefolia) 5' by 2'
Phlox, variegated summer
Plume poppy (Macleaya cordata) 8' by 3'
Prairie blazing-star (Liatris pycnostachya) 4' purple
        blooms July to September
Queen-of-the-prairie (Filipendula rubra) 7' pink
        blooms June to August
Russian sage (Perovskia atriplicifolia),
Rocket series Sunflower, Maximillian (Healianthus
        maximillani) 9', yellow blooms August to
        October or perennial sunflower (Helianthus x
        multiflorus) 8' by 3'
Sneezeweed (Helenium autumnale),
Stiff goldenrod (Solidago rigida) 5' yellow blooms July
        to October
Turk's cap lily (Lillium superbum) 8' orange flowers
        July to August
Yarrow (Achillea filipendulina 'Gold Plate'),
Zebra grass (M.s. 'Zebrinus')

Medium Sized plants

Asters
Astilbe spp and cvs (Astilbe)
Black-eyed susan (Rudbecia fulgida)
Cosmos, Sonata series
Daylily cvs (Hemerocallis x hybrida)
Iceland poppies Champagne Bubbles strain (Papaver
        nudicaule)
False Sunflower (Heliopsis helianthoides)
Fountain grass (Pennisetum alopecuroides) 4' by 2'
Gloriosa daisies (Rudbeckia hirta)
Japanese anemone cvs. (Anemone x hybrida)
Lamb's ears (Stachys byzantina)
Penstemons 'Apple Blossom' and 'Firebird'
Sedum Stonecrop (Sedum 'Autumn Joy'
Sneezeweed (Helenium 'Moerheim Beauty') 3' by 2'
Yarrow 'Salmon Beauty' (Achillea)

Fillers for the fronts of borders

Chrysanthemum paludosum
Coreopsis cvs. (C. verticillata)
Lamb's ears (Stachys byzantina) 18" by 2'
Lilyturf (Lirope muscari 'Variegata')
Pansies
Scabiosa 'Butterfly Blue'
Silvermound (Artemisia schmidtiana) 1' by 18"
Star-of-Bethlehem (Ornithogalum nutans)
Sweet allysums (Lobularia maritime)
Thrift (Armeria maritime)
Violas
Wood sorrel (Oxalis spp.)

Fall Color

Amur Maple (Acer ginnala) - brilliant red – 'Compacta', 'Flame', 'Red Rhapsody' 6' to 20'

Aster 'Purple Dome' and wormwood (Artemisia x "Powis Castle')

Barberry (Berberis thunbergii) – brilliant red – 'Artopurpurea', 'Crimson Pygmy' and 'Rose Glow.' Height varies.

Black-eyed Susan (Rudbeckia fulgida) 'Goldsturm' 2' blooms from June to frost or (r. hirta) 'Indian Summer' 6"-9"

Blueberry (Vaccinium corymbosum) – scarlet or yellow. Plant two for pollination. Acid soil. 5' to 6' or more.

Bridalwreath (Spiraea prunifolia) 'Plena'

burning bush

Winged euonymus (E. alata) – glowing rose red 10' 'Compacta' to 6'

Chrysanthemums

Common Sneezeweed (Helenium autumnale)

Disanthus (D. cercidifolius) – intense orange, red, and purple, 8' to 15'

Enkianthus (E. campanulatus) – brilliant yellow to red, acid loving, 10'

Eulalia grass (Miscanthus sinensis) 5'-6' ; 'Yaku Jima' 3'-4' sun or shade

Fothergilla (F. gardenia, F. major) yellow to scarlet, 2' to 10' also Fothergilla major

Grape, gloryvine (Vitis vinifera 'Purpurea', V. coignetiae) – bright yellow, orange, red, and purple – vigorous vine 10' to 50'

Heather (Calluna vulgaris) 'Wickwar Flame'

Japanese Maple (A. palmatum) – golden or crimson – 'Crimson Queen', Dissectum', 'Ever Red', ' Ornatum' 5' to 7', 'Osakazuki'

Oakleaf Hydrangea (H. quercifolia 'Snow queen') –
crimson, purple, or bronze 6'
Rosa rugosa 'Rote's Meer', 3.5' to 4' purply flowers
good fall foliage, 'Fru Dagmar Hastrup' 4' best
fall colors of yellows, oranges, and scarlets.
Sedum 'Autumn Joy' with Lavatera trimestris 'Silver
Cup'
Spiraea (S. bumalda) – coppery orange, red, or
burgundy 'Froebelii', 'Goldflame', or
'Goldmound' – 2' to 3'
Summersweet (Clethera alnifolia) bright
yellow, 10'
Sumac (Rhus glabra, R. typhina – brilliant
scarlet . 10' to 15'
Tartarian dogwood (Cornus alba) 'Sibirica'
Verbena bonariensis with Cleome hassleriana
Viburnum – purplish red or bright red. Height varies.
Witch hazel (Hamamelis vernalis) 'Sandra'- 10' to 15'
Winter hazel (Corylopsis) – yellow 8' to 10'

Trees
Acer palmatum 'Bloodgood', 'Omato' (red)
'Osakazuki' (red) 'Hogyoku' (orange to gold),
'Ichigyoji' (gold to orange), 'Green Star' (red,
orange, and gold), and 'kogane Sakae' (red,
orange, and gold). 15'
Laceleafs: 'Filigree' 6', yellow: Orangeola 7', flame red:
and 'Seiryu 12', red, orange, and gold
Betula jacquemontii (Himalayan birch)

Shrubs
'Glow' Dwarf mugho pine (Pinus mugo pumillio)
Japanese barberry 'Rose'
Scotch heather (calluna vulgaris) 'David
Eason' (mauve) or 'Finale' (rosy purple).

Combinations

Coleus 'Alabama Sunset' (annual) with burgundy dahlia
       'Burma Gem', orange amaranthus, and
       golden-leaved barberry
Solidago Canadensis with New England asters
Orange Calluna vulgaris 'Wickwar Flame' with Spiraea
       japonica 'Anthony Waterer'
Fothergilla major and silvery Pittosporum tenuifolium
       'Irene Paterson'
Kamchatka bugbane (Cimicufuga simplex) and
       black-flowering sedge (Carex nigra)
Anemone x hybrida 'Honorine Jobert', Verbena
       bonariensis and Aster frikartii
Sedum 'Autumn Joy' and Pennisetum setaceum
'Rubrum' or pink cleome and golden rudbeckia

Fall Cutting Garden

Aster (Aster novae-angliae) 'Purple Dome' (6) plants
18" by 18" purple.
Dahlia (Dahlia pinnata) Redskin Mix (12) 18" by 12"
Fountain grass (Pennisetum setaceum) 'Rubrum' (1),
3' by 24"
Goldenrod (Solidago) 'Crown of Rays' (6) 2' by 18"
Helen's flower (Helenium autumnale) 'Kugelsonne' (2)
       4' by 2' yellow or 'Moerheim Beauty' (2) 4' by
       2' red
Love-in-a-mist (Nigella damascene) (10) 12" by 6"
       Annual, re-seeds itself.

Zinnia (Zinnia Thumbelina hybrids) (10) 10" by 6"
Mixed hues. Annual.
Zinnia Dreamland hybrids (10) 12" by 4" Annual

Fall Foliage Border

Purple Coneflower (Echinacea purpurea) (6)
Autumn Joy Stonecrop (3)
Purple Fountain Grass (Pennisetum setaceum)
        'Rubrum' (1)
Royal Purple Smoke Tree (Cotinus coggygria) 'Royal
        Purple' (2)
Cranberry Cotoneaster (3)
Bloodgood Japanese Maple (Acer palmatum)
        'Bloodgood' (1)
Heavenly Bamboo (Nandina Domestica) 'Monum'(1)
        and 'Firepower' (1)
Red Leaf Japanese Barberry (Berberis thunbergii)
        'Atropurpurea' (2)
Heuchera Coral Bells (Heuchera Micrantha)
        'Palace Purple' (3)

Winter color

Bamboo (Pleioblastis auricomus)
Blue spruce (Picea pungens)
Cedrus atlantica 'Glauca' and C. deodara
Chinese Paper birch (Betula albosinensis)
Chinese witch hazel (Hamamelis mollis 'Pallida') 15'
Cotoneaster
Daphne Einter (C. odora 'Aureomarginata')
Early spiketail (Stachyurus praecox)
Filberts Harry Lauder's walking stick (Corylus
        'Contorta')
Hollie (Ilex opaca, l.x attenuate, and I. pedunculosa)
Japanese umbrella pine (Sciadopitys verticillata)
Mahonia 'Arthur Menzies'
Nandina 'Gulf Stream' 3', 'Harbour Dwarf 2', 'Moyers
        Red' 5', 'Nana' 1' and 'Umpqua Warrior 4'.
        Plant in November.
Pyracantha
Redosier dogwood
Redtwig dogwoods
Heather (Calluna vulgaris)
Rhododendrons
Silk-tassel bush (garrya elliptica)
Skimmia

Winter Combinations
Miscanthus grass with New Zealand flax (Phormium)
        and fountain grass (Pennisetum
        alopecuroides)
Eulalia grass (Miscanthus sinensis) with Japanese
        barberry (Berberis thunbergii 'Crimson
        Pygmy')

Winterberry (ilex verticillata 'Harvest Red' with
        fountain grass and Russian sage (Perovski
        atriplicifolia).
Redosier dogwood (Cornus sericea) and winterberry
        (Ilex verticillata)
Bear's foot hellebore (Hellebore foetidus) and snow
        drops (Galanthus nivalis)
Sunoymus fortunei 'Emerald Gaiety' and Hinoki false
        cypress (Chamaecyparis obtusa)
Yucca filamentosa 'Golden Sword' and Sawara false
        cypress (Chamaecyparis pisifera 'Golden Mop'
Weeping Pinus strobes 'Pendula' and mounding
        blue-gray Genista Lydia
Acacia with Almond, Camellia, flowering plum and
        Polyanthus jasmine (Jasminum polyanthum)

All-Season Interest

<u>**Trees:**</u>
Cryptomeria japonica 'Elegans' (plume cedar)
Eucalyptus pauciflora niphophila (snow gum)
Picea pungens 'Bakeri' (Baker's blue spruce)

<u>**Shrubs:**</u>
Mahonia 'Arthur Menzies'
Pieris japonica 'Mountain Fire'

<u>**Vines**</u>
Blueberry climber (Ampelopsis brevipedunculata)
Clematis (C. alpine or macropetala 'Bluebird')
Golden hops (Humulus lupulus)
Hedera canariensis 'Gloire de Marengo'
Kiwi vine (Actinidia)
Morning glory (Ipomoea)
Parthenocissus henryana (silvervein creeper)
Vitis vinifera 'Purpurea' (purple-leafed grape)
Wisteria

<u>**Grasses:**</u>
Calamagrostis arundinacea 'Karl Foerster'
Helictotrichon sempervirens (blue oat grass)
Miscanthus sinensis 'Cosmopolitan'

Fairy Garden Plants

Agapanthus 'Tinkerbell'
Astilbe simplicifolia 'Sprite' 18"
Baby's breath (Gypsophila paniculata 'Bristol Fairy' 3'
Erigeron speciosus 'Azure Fairy' 18"
Fairy primrose (Primula malacoides)
Fairy thimble (Campanula cochlearifolia 'Bavarian Blue'
        10"
Fuschia 'Fairy Earrings' cascading
Geranium 'Fairy Magic' 8"
Gomphrena Gnome Mix – annual
Heuchera 'Petite Pearl Fairy' 6"
Lavendula angustifolia 'Fairy Pink' 18"
Phygelius x rectus 'Pink Elf' 3'

Plants for Attracting Butterflies

Spring

Aubretia – ground cover, perennial
Candytuft (Iberis spp.) low evergreen ground cover
Clematis spp. Vine
Columbine (Aquilegia spp.)
Coral bells (Heuchera sanguinea) low perennial
Lavender (Lavandula spp.)
Lilac (Syringa spp.) shrub
Marigold (Tagetes) annual
Pinks (Dianthus spp.)
Primrose (Primula spp.)
Rockcress (Arabis spp.) low, flowering perennial

Summer

Butterfly bush (Buddleia spp.)
Butterfly weed (asclepius tuberose) Perennial
Clematis spp.
Heliotrope (Heliotropum arborescens)
Hollyhock (Alcea spp.) biennial
Honeysuckle (Lonicera spp.) vine
Lilies (Lilium spp.)
Marigold (Tagetes) annual
Nicotiana spp. Annual
Petunia spp. Annual
Phlox spp. Perennials and annuals
Purple coneflower (Echinacea spp.) perennial
Verbena spp.

Fall

Aster spp. Perennial
Bluebeard (Caryopteris spp.) blue flowers
Goldenrod (Solidago spp.) Medium perennial, gold
        blooms.
Marigold (Tagetes spp.) annual
Petunia spp.
Phlox spp.
Purple coneflower (Echinacea purpurea) takes drought.
Stonecrop (Sedum spectabile)

Plants for Attracting Hummingbirds

Beard-tongue (Penstemon spp.)
Bee balm (Monarda didyma)
Begonia (Begonia spp.)
Bugleweed (Ajuga spp.) ground cover, blue flowers in
     May
Bleeding heart (Dicentra spp.)
Coral bells (Heuchera spp.)
Fuchsia
Honeysuckle (Lonicera spp.) vine
Lilies (Lilium spp.)
Phlox (Phlox spp.)
Purple coneflower (Echinacea purpurea) purple and
     white summer flowers
Rosemary (Rosmarinus officinalis) herb with blue
     flowers
Sage (Salvia spp.) herb, low-growing
Weigela (Weigela spp.)

All-Season Pots

Keep texture and color repetition in mind. Repeat the
color of the upright elements in trailing plants.
Choose a pot at least 14 inches deep and 16 inches
across --- for larger plantings should be 32 inches
across. The sample:
2 Nandinas
2 'Rainbow' Leucothoes
2 Pampas Grass plants
2 Euonmus 'Silver Queen'
a green Santolina
Salal
Ribbon grass
2 'Peacock' Kale and
5 Pansies planted over 10 Tulip bulbs.

Put the main plants in the pot. In the fall add the bulbs
and violas or flowering kale. In February replace the
fall annuals with primroses. In early spring plant
lobelia, ageratum, geraniums, marigolds, or petunias.

Other variations: Mexican orange, azalea, and mahonia;
or nandina, mahonia, and flax with pink azalea
golden viola, and peach-colored Primula obconica.
After the tulips fade, add French marigolds, zinnias, and
gaillardia.

In a great big urn, plant canna lilies, abutilon, begonias,
fuschia, and heliotrope.
Or plant asparagus fern, lotus vine with sweet potato
vine in chartreuse or maroon.

Heliotrope and geraniums are pot staples.
In jewel-toned pots, plant verbena, heliotrope,
chocolate cosmos, purple fountain grass, and coleus.

Spring Pots

In the fall, plant a corkscrew hazel (Corylus avellana
'Contorta') in a pot with bulbs. Or false holly
(Osmanthus heterophyllus 'Goshiki') with bacopa and
crocus. Put the tree in the pot first. Put the latest
blooming spring bulbs on the bottom –halfway down
the pot. (ruffled pink Angelique or deeper pink May
Wonder) Use 7 to 9 bulbs – as many as you can
squeeze in without touching each other or the sides of
the pot. Fill in around them. Add bulb food and cover
with a few inches of soil. Then add a layer of
mid-season bulbs like hyacinths or narcissus. Fill in
with soil again and add a top layer of early blooming
crocus, grape hyacinth or iris reticulate. In the top
layer of soil add ground covers, winter pansies, little
ornamental grasses, Heucheras, or bronze sedge Carex
comans to droop down the pot.

In a 23" diameter pot, plant 10 daffodils, 10 tulips, 7
pansies, a pair of sedges, 2 Euphorbia purpurea and
gallon-sized Hypericum 'Albury Purple' and Leucothoe
fontanesiana 'Rainbow.'

Other bulbs that like pots: Lily of the Nile (Agapanthus
africanus), Caladium (Caladium bicolor), Pineapple lily
(Eucomis bicolor), Jacobean lily (Sprekelia
formosissima), Mexican shell flower (Tigridia pavonia),
Tuberous begonia (Begonia x tuberhybrida).

Summer Pots

Begonia
Caladium
Croton
Dahlias, rose and yellow double-flowered
Geranium
Kalanchoe
Lantana
Marguerites
Mullein
Nasturtium
New Zealand flax
Ornamental grasses
Petunias,
Plume Poppy
Portulaca
Red Salvia
Rue
Sweet Alyssum
Zinnia

Combinations:
'Myers' asparagus with Dusty Miller
Dracaena marginata with Coleus
Dusty miller with French Marigolds and Lobelia
Tuberous Begonias with Lobelia
Fuschia 'Firecracker' with Helichrysum petiolare

Herb Pot: 1 bronze fennel, 1 marjoram, 1 chive, 1 mint, 1 parsley, 1 thyme, 1 rosemary in one 14" container.

Sun combination:
2 bacopa (Sutera 'Snowfalls'), 1 Osteospermum 'Lemon
Symphony', 1 Osteospermum 'Orange Symphony', 1
Streptocarpella (Streptocarpus 'Concord Blue' in a 10"
container

Part shade combinations:

3 white petunias (Petunia grandiflora) with 1 Sweet
potato vine (Ipomoea batatas'Marguerite'), 2
geraniums (Pelargonium 'Frank Headley') and one
Astilbe chinensis (taquetii 'Superba')

3 bacopa (Sutera Snowstorm brand), 1 trailing
snapdragon (Antirrhinum majus Luminaire yellow and
1 trailing snapdragon (Antirrhinum majus Luminaire
Hot Pink), 1 osteospermum 'Lemon Symphony',
2 Calibrachoa Million Bells Terra Cotta , 1 verbena
Aztec Silver Magic in one 14" hanging basket.

1 spiderwort (Tradescantia 'Sweet Kate'), 2 Sweet
potato vines (Ipomoea babatas 'Marguerite'), 2
geranium (Pelargonium Designer Hot Coral), 3 licorice
vine (Helichrysum petiolare) and 2
Osteospermum 'Lemon Symphony' in a 14" container.

Tall and trailing: 1 coreopsis 'Moonbeam', 2 trailing
snapdragon (Antirrhinum majus Luminaire Harvest
Red), 3 licorice vine (Helichrysum petiolare) 2 coleus
(Solenostemon scutellarioides Aurora Stoplight) in a
16" container.

Pink in the shade: 2 trailing coleus (Solenostemon
scutellarioides 'Trailing Rose', 3 Verbena Aztec Hot
Pink , 3 Calibrachoa Million Bells Cherry Pink in a 14"
hanging basket.

Full sun combinations:

2 trailing snapdragons (Antirrhinum majus Luminaire Yellow) with 3 Calibrachoa Milllion Bells Deep Blue and 3 Verbena Aztec Red.

1 Mandevilla splendens, 4 Osteospermum 'Vanilla Symphony', 2 Verbena Aztec Cherry Red, 2 Scaevola aemula, 2 Calibrachoa Million Bells Cherry Red and 2 Calibrachoa Million Bells Terra Cotta

Autumn Pots

Mid-season tulips (orange and purple 'Princess Irene'), Iris reticulata, heuchera, heather, hebes, pansies, hellebores and euphorbia. Center with an evergreen fern, camellia or nandina.
Other small conifers are: Crytomeria japonica 'Tansu', yellow thuja orientalis 'Aurea Nana' and the silver-blue Juniperus horizontalis 'Blue Pygmy.'
Prostanthera rotunndifolia 4'-6' or round-leaf-mint bush, bay laurel or rosemary.
Rhodendron 'PJM' has a purple cast in winter.
Rhodendron Dora Amateis.
Deciduous trees: Corylus avellana (corkscrew hazel) or Acer palmatum (Japanese maple), hazelnut
Can also add Fuschia magellanica (hardy fuschia), bergenia.
Finish the top of the pot with galanthus, snowdrops, and grape hyacinth, crocus.

Try planting these together:

Variegated Hebe (H.x ranciscana) 'Variegata'
 Michelmas daisies (Aster novibelgii)
Sedum 'Matrona'
Artemisia 'Powis Castle'
Burgundy fountain grass (Pennisetum setaceum)
'Purpureum'.

Or try this combination:

Coleus 'Alabama Sunset'
Centurea gymnocarpa
Arctotis 'Rosita'
Petunia integrifolia 'TNT'
Alternanthera dentate 'Rubiginosa'
Agastache spp.

Perennial Pots

Plants for Height:

Abutila
Artemisia (A. ludoviciana albula 'Silver king')
       silver-gray to white. 3'
Aster (A. frikartii) 3' yellow centered blue flowers
Aucuba
Baby's breath (Gypsophila paniculate) 'Bristol Fairy', 3',
       white flowers
Caladium
Chrysanthemum pacificum 2' gold flowers – looks good
       all year
Croton
Cupid's dart (Catananche caerulea) grass-like foliage 2'
       blue flowers
Dieffenbachia
Dracaena marginata
Ferns, lace and upright
Fountain grass (Pennisetum setaceum) 'Rubrum'
       purple foliage, 3', pink, red and white flowers
       or (alopecurioides) 3', pink flowers. 'Hameln'
       is 2'
Fox red curly sedge (Carex buchananii) red-bronze 2'
Fuschia 'Gartenmeister Bonstedt'
Gloriosa daisy (Rudbeckia hirta) 3' summer to fall. R.
       fulgida 'Goldsturm' is longer lived.
Helianthus angustifolius 6', 2" yellow flowers
Jerusalem sage (Phlomis fruticosa) gray-green leaves to
       3'. Bright yellow flowers in late spring.
Kangaroo paw (Anigozanthos flavidus) 3' Fuzzy red,
       yellow, or chartreuse flowers bloom spring to

Mullein (Verbascum) 1', white flowers on V. chaixii
      'Album'; yellow flowers on V. bombyciferum
      'Arctic Summer'
Nandina 'Gulf Stream'
New Zealand flax (Phormium tenax) 5' bronze, red,
      purple. Looks good all year.
Palms
Penstemon, 3'-6', pink, red, white, purple flowers in fall
Plume poppy (Macleaya cordata) 8', bluish green leaves
Purple coneflower (Echinacea purpurea) 3'-5' Rosy
      purple flowers
Rue (Ruta graveolens) 3' looks good all year
Verbena bonariensis 5' purple flowers

Fillers and Bloomers

Annuals: Besides the usual Petunias and Lobelia, try
Browallia, Coleus, Impatiens, Kalanchoe, Pink polka-dot
plant, Rieger begonia
Begonias
Calceolaria
Dusty Miller
Ferns
Hosta
Hydrangeas
Liriope 'Majestic'
Myers' asparagus
Pincushion flower (Scabiosa columbaria anthemifolia)
      1.5' blue flowers most of the year
Sage (Salvia) 1'-5' with blue, purple, red, or white
      flowers.
Sedum (S. telephium)'Autumn Joy' 2' pink flowers fade
      to copper

Cascaders and drapers

Asteriscus maritimus 'Gold Coin' 1' golden daisies
summer through fall
Catmint (Nepeta faassenii) 'Six Hills Giant' 3' gray
foliage with blue flowers
Creeping fig (ficus pumila)
Grape ivy
Japanese sedge (Carex morrowii expallida) 1'. Looks
good all year.
Lamb's ears (Stachys byzantina) 1.5'
Lamium 'White Nancy' or 'Beacon Silver'
Lavender cotton (Santolina chamaecyparissus) 2'
yellow flowers
Lemon Thyme (Thymus citriodorus) 1', pale purple
flowers in summer.
Licorice plant (Helichrysum petiolatum) 2', silver gray
foliage
Lobelia (annual)
Moneywort
Sedum S. sieboldii 'Ruby Glow' blue-green leaves, with
red flowers in late summer; S. spurium 8" with
green to bronze leaves and pink flowers in
summer
Sweet Woodruff
Twinspur (Diascia) 1.5' pink flowers in spring and
summer
Vinca minor

Shaded Pots

Agapanthus
Astilbes
Aspidistra
Begonias
Browallia
Caladium
Calla
Coleus
Cyclamen
Diefenbachia
Fuschia 'Gartenmeister Bonstedt'
Hosta
Impatiens
Liriope
Sweet alyssum
Sweet Woodruff

Rhododendrons

R. campylogynum – dwarf alpine with thimble shaped
  pink to purple flowers
R. degronianum ssp. Yakushimanum –mounding dwarf
  with pink buds that open to white flowers
R. hodgsonii – rose-purple flowers and peeling reddish
  bark
R. luteum 'Golden Comet' – deciduous azaleas with
  deep-yellow flowers and bright-red foliage
R. oreotrephes – blue-green to olive foliage and masses
  of lavender to red-purple flowers
R. pseudochrysanthum – silvery leaves, pink buds,
  white flowers. Sun and shade tolerant.
R. russatum – dwarf alpine with dark purple flowers.
  Tolerant of full sun.
R. williamsianum – mounding with rosy-pink flowers
  'Blue Diamond' and R. pachysanthum perform
  well in the sun.

Combinations:

Plant a R.'Unique' apricot with a Kousa dogwood
  (Cornus kousa)

Combine rhododendrons with conifers, New Zealand
  flax, or Fatsia Japonica, ajuga, Colorado blue
  spruce, or a Japanese maple.

Hebe elliptica 'Variegata', hostas, and Solomon's seal
  (Polygonatum odoratum) 'Variegatum', and
  'Elijah Blue' fescue are also good additions.

Roses

Best for the Northwest Hybrid Teas:
Election, Just Joey, Keepsake, Las Vegas, Olympiad,
Silver Jubilee, Voo Doo

Best for the Northwest Floribundas:
Class Act, Europeana, Impatient, Liverpool Echo,
Matangi, Playboy, Reginsberg, Sarabande, Show Biz,
Trumpeter, Viva

Best for the Northwest climbing roses: Dortmund,
Dublin Bay, Royal Sunset.

Best for the Northwest Grandifloras: Love,
Tournament of Roses, Rosa mulliganii, 'Gemini,
'Fragrant Apricot', 'Vanilla Perfume'

Best for color: 'Barbara Streisand' lavender, 'First
Kiss' pink, "Full Sail' white, 'Gold Medal' gold,
'Olympiad' red, and 'Timeless' rose pink

Best for Fragrance: 'Voodoo' orange and 'Sombreuil'
white

Rose Ground Covers: Alba Meidiland, Mox Graf, Magic
Carpet, Magic Meidiland, 'The Fairy', Rosa Paulii, Rosa
rugosa 'Charles Alanel' 1.5' – carpet

Attractive Foliage: 'Belle Story,' 'Buff Beauty,' 'Cerise
Bouquet,' 'Pleasure,' Rosa glauca, Rosa hugonis, Rosa
rugosa

Disease Resistant: 'Agnes,'Bonica', 'Buff Beauty', 'Charles de Mills', 'Complicata', 'Constance Spry', 'Dortmund', 'The Fairy', 'French Lace', 'Harison's Yellow', 'Mme. Hardy', 'Morning Jewel',

Waterwise: 'Buff Beauty', 'Dortmund', 'La Sevillana', 'The Fairy', 'Fibriata', 'Fruhlingsgold,' 'Pretty Jessica', Rosa eglaneria, Rosa glauca, Rosa rugosa, and many groundcover roses.

Shade tolerant: 'Agnes' Albas', 'Cerise Bouquet', 'Complicata', 'Harrison's Yellow', 'Iceberg', 'Marjorie Fair', 'Pax', 'Scarlet Meidiland'

Rose spray for blackspot --- I TBSP bicarbonate of soda in a gallon of water. There are also a number of commercial options. Blackspot and mildew form a resistance to any particular spray, so be sure to vary whatever you use.

Underplant roses with violets, pansies, auricular primroses, lamb's ears (Stachys lanata or Stachy byzantina, artemisias, lavender cottons (Santolina chamaecyparissus) and campanulas.

Combinations: the pink climbing rose 'Mme. Sancy de Parabere' with mauvy-purple Clematis 'Mrs. P.T. James' or apricot-pink R. 'Buff Beauty' with violet Clematis viticella 'Purpurea Plena Elegans'.

Ornamental Grasses

Sunny spots

Black mondo grass (Ophiogogon planiscapus) small
      tufts of black leaves form a good groundcover

Blue hair grass (Koeleria glauca) small mounder with
      blue leaves

Blue Lyme grass (Elymus magellanicus) narrow blue
      leaves

Carex buchananii - bronze, 18", grow with Bergenia

Carex morrowii expallida (also called "variegate")

Drooping sedge (Carex pendula)

Eulalia grass (Miscanthus sinensis) 8', white blooms
      August to September

Feather grass (Stipa gigantean) yellow flowers in
      summer

Feather reed grass (Calamagrostis acutiflora) 'Stricta'

Fescue (Festuca scoparia) 'Pic Carlit' small mounder

Festuca glauca or Common Blue Fescue

Fountain grass (Pennisetum alopecuroides) 4' by 2',

Giant miscanthus (Miscanthus floridulus) tall clumper
      with fall flowers

Narrow feather grass (S. tenuissima) showy brown in
      late summer.

Pampas grass (Cortaderia selloana)

Part shade

Black Mondo Grass (Ophiopogon planiscarpus) – nice
      edge to a walkway

Blue sedge (Carex glauca) likes dry shade

Helictotrichon aparicus nanus

Japanese Blood Grass (Imperata cylindrical aka
Miscanthus floridulus)

Japanese Forest Grass (Hakonechloa macra)

Vines

Fast-growing, flowering annual vines:

Black-eyed Susan vine (Thunbergia alata) 8', orange,
yellow or white flowers
Cup-and-saucer vine (Cobea scandens) 10" to 25', large
violet or white flowers
Cypress vine or cardinal climber (Ipomoea quamoclit)
to 20', feathery foliage, 1" wide scarlet flowers
Hyacinth bean (Lablab purpureus) 10' or more,
fragrant white or purple flowers
Moonflower (Ipomoea alba) 8' to 10', huge perfumed,
night-blooming white flowers
Morning glory (Ipomoea spp.)

Perennial Vines:

Blueberry climber (Ampelopsis) 15' sun or shade, blue
berries in the fall
Climbing roses
Clematis (Clematis alpine) or (Clematis macropetala
'Bluebird')
Climbing hydrangea (Hydrangea petiolaris) 60'
Golden hops (Humulus lupulus) 20' in a season. Needs
lots of sun and water.
Wisteria (Wisteria spp) 30 –40'
Hardy kiwi (Actinidia arguta) to 50'

Annuals

Castor bean (Ricinus communis) 6' by 3'
Celosia Century series, 18" by 6"
Cleome (Cleome hassleriana) 5' pink to lavender
     blooms partial shade to hot sun. Self seeding.
Cupflower (Nierembergia) 'Mont Blanc' 8" by 8"
Four o'clock (Mirabilis jalapa 'Alba') 2'
Gomphrena 'Strawberry Fields', 30" by 1'
Jasmine tobacco (Nicotiana alata 'Grandiflora' and N.
     sylvestris) 5'self-sowing annuals
Mexican sunflower (Tithonia rotundifolia) 3'-4'
     Drought and heat resistant. Self seeds.
Morning glory (Ipomoea purpurea) 15' to 20', 2" blue,
     purple, pink, or white flowers.
Nasturtiums (Tropaeolum majus)
Phlox (Phlox drummondii)
Prince's feather (amaranthus cruentus) 6' by 18"
Night-scented stock (Matthiola longipetala, formerly M.
     bicornis) 1' lavender and white blooms.
     (annual)
Zinnia 'California Giants', 3' by 6"
Melampodium 1' by 1'
Marigolds
Schizanthus or poor man's orchid
Petunias

Made in the USA
Coppell, TX
07 December 2022

88058794R00066